Who is my neighbour?

A Letter from the House of Bishops to the People and Parishes of the Church of England for the General Election 2015

THE CHURCH OF ENGLAND

Whatever is true, whatever is honourable, whatever is just, whatever is pure, whatever is pleasing, whatever is commendable, if there is any excellence and if there is anything worthy of praise, think about these things.

Philippians 4:8

How should Christian men and women approach the General Election to be held on 7 May 2015? This letter from the Church of England's House of Bishops is addressed to all members of the church. And, as the Church of England strives to be a church which seeks the good of all the people of the country, we hope that others, who may not profess church allegiance, will nevertheless join in the conversation and engage with the ideas we are sharing here.

This letter is not a shopping list of policies we would like to see. It is a call for the new direction that we believe our political life ought to take.

Who is my Neighbour?

1   We live in challenging but hopeful times. All political parties struggle to communicate a convincing vision. People feel detached from politics. Alongside a healthy openness to new ideas, worrying and unfamiliar trends are appearing in our national life. There is a growing appetite to exploit grievances, find scapegoats and create barriers between people and nations. The issues around the election call for a fresh moral vision of the kind of country we want to be.

2   Followers of Jesus Christ believe that every human being is created in the image of God. But we are not made in isolation. We belong together in a creation which should be cherished and not simply used and consumed. This is the starting point for the Church of England's engagement with society, the nation and the world. All that we say here follows from this. Anglicans do not have a single view on which political party has the best mix of answers to today's problems. As bishops we support policies which respect the natural environment, enhance human dignity and honour the image of God in our neighbour.

> As bishops we support policies which respect the natural environment, enhance human dignity and honour the image of God in our neighbour.

3   The General Election on 7 May 2015 is the first for which the date
     has been set so long in advance. We have an unprecedented
     opportunity to think through the issues that face the nation and
     to ensure that the concerns and insights of the Christian gospel
     are reflected in the debates that will help shape the outcome. This
     letter is intended to help church members and others consider the
     question: how can we negotiate these dangerous times to build the
     kind of society which many people say they want but which is not yet
     being expressed in the vision of any of the parties?

4   We are suggesting the trajectory for a new kind of politics – one
     which works constructively with a ferment of different ideas and
     competing visions. Although we have numerous specific concerns
     about particular issues in national life today – and will no doubt be
     developing those ideas in other places – here we want to move
     beyond flagging up lists of issues to dig deeper into questions about
     the trajectory of our political life and visions of the kind of society
     we want to be and which political life should serve. If anyone claims
     that this letter is "really" saying "Vote for this party or that party", they
     have misunderstood it.

5   The privileges of living in a democracy mean that we should use our
     votes thoughtfully, prayerfully, and with the good of others in mind,
     not just our own interests. Pursuing the common good is a Christian
     obligation and is expressed in how we approach our role as voters as
     much as in our personal priorities.

Christian faith and political activity

6   Some people, including some in the positions of influence in the media, politics and elsewhere, claim that religion and politics cannot mix. They assert that religion belongs solely to the private sphere and must not trespass into the realm of political or economic life. Although this is often treated as a universal truth, it is a view largely confined to the modern-day European context. In previous centuries, and in most parts of the world today, it has been accepted that religious belief of its nature addresses the whole of life, private and public. It is not possible to separate the way a person perceives his or her place in the created order from their beliefs, religious or otherwise, about how the world's affairs ought to be arranged.

7   The claim that religion and political life must be kept separate is, in any case, frequently disingenuous – most politicians and pundits are happy enough for the

> religious belief, of its nature, addresses the whole of life, private and public.

churches to speak on political issues so long as the church agrees with their particular line. But Christian engagement with political issues has to go deeper than aligning the church with one party, policy, or ideology.

8   Observers of the global scene will recognise that religion, far from withering on the vine as urbanisation, industrialisation, wealth and education increase (the theory of secularisation), has a growing public profile and cannot be ignored as a political force. Without a grasp of the power and meaning of religion, it is impossible to understand the dynamics of global politics today.

> The challenge to politicians is to understand how faith can shape communities, nations and individuals for the good.

9   Some of this resurgent religion has been harmful. It is a mistake to imagine that all manifestations of religion are essentially similar or always benign. But the challenge to politicians is to understand how faith can shape communities, nations and individuals for the good. The answer to "furious religion" (that is, the religious impulse turned in on itself or used to justify oppression and conflict) is not to marginalise religion in general or see religious faith as some kind of problem. It is to acknowledge that religious commitment is extraordinarily widespread and that people of faith within all the historic traditions have much to offer to a vision of a good society and a peaceful world.

A Christian world-view

10 Christianity is an incarnational faith – Jesus Christ lived as one of us, shared the joys and hardships of ordinary life and died a violent and shameful death. Wherever we find ourselves, he has shared our condition. His resurrection is a sign that the sufferings of the world are not the last word and that God's transforming power can turn the material world – not just the spiritual – to work for good. Christians believe that we are called to share in this responsibility for bringing to birth a new creation.

11 Christ's incarnation confirms the fundamental truth that every human being is created in the image of God. Because of this, we are called to love our neighbour as ourselves. This is the starting point for all of the church's engagement with society, politics and national life. This is the truth that lies behind everything we have to say here.

12 Christians everywhere and throughout the ages have prayed, as part of The Lord's Prayer, "Thy Kingdom Come, Thy will be done, on earth as in heaven". That is why politics and the life of the Christian disciple cannot be separated. That is why the church calls its members to play a full part in the political life of the nation and to support politicians and the government with their prayers.

13 Jesus said, "I came that they might have life, and have it abundantly"
(John 10). A Christian approach to politics must be driven by this vision:
enabling all people to live good lives, with the chance to realise their
potential, as individuals and together as a people.

14 Christians take sin
seriously. It is impossible
for us to be starry-eyed
about the potential of
politics to perfect the
social order or adequately
reflect the Kingdom of
God. To speak of human
sin is not the same as
apportioning blame and
being judgemental. All
are sinners; all fall short.

> We should neither hold politicians to a higher set of moral standards than we expect from ourselves, nor allow them off the hook by treating political life as if it were outside the demands of morality.

We should neither hold politicians to a higher set of moral standards
than we expect from ourselves, nor allow them off the hook by
treating political life as if it were outside the demands of morality.

15 But while we take sin seriously, the greater truth at the heart of the
gospel is about repentance and salvation. Repentance starts with
the acknowledgement that all is not well, that what is good and
right has been neglected and that change is inescapable. Salvation
follows from the atoning work of Christ – literally making things "at
one" with each other and with God.

16   Christians believe that God alone is Lord of creation and our allegiance to any other system or power is only possible so long as it makes no claims which compromise our allegiance to God. Christians should be wary of accumulations of power wherever they take place. They should be as reluctant to live under an overweening corporate sector as under an overweening state. Where the state or the market, or any other powers, claim too much and stifle human flourishing, people are divided from one another and God's sovereignty is mocked.

17   "Put not your trust in princes", says the Psalmist (Ps.146). The prophets speak out against traders who seek only profit and upset the rhythms of community life by their greed (Amos 8). Jesus is harsh towards leaders (including religious leaders) who seek power and privilege and neglect justice and mercy for others (Matthew 23). The Biblical tradition is not only "biased to the poor", as often noted, but warns constantly against too much power falling into too few hands. When it does, human sympathies are strained to breaking point.

18   These theological insights are as relevant to political and public life as they are to people's personal lives. Our nation faces deep divisions and the gulfs between people and communities seem to be widening. At-one-ment is as necessary a goal for public life as it is for the personal dimension.

19 Looked at through the prism of Christian theology, the state of the
    world today reflects the fact that we live "between the times" – in
    a world where the Holy Spirit is alive and active, yet a world still
    characterised by the persistence of sin. Because grace and sin are
    in tension in everyone, claims to have grasped ultimate truth for all
    time, whether in theology, politics, economics or anything else, are
    bound to be wrong.

20 None of us has a "God's-
    eye view". It behoves
    all people, including
    politicians, church leaders
    and opinion formers, to
    "think it possible that you
    may be mistaken" – to
    use the words of Oliver
    Cromwell.

> the church has an obligation to engage constructively with the political process, and Christians share responsibility with all citizens to participate in the democratic structures of our nation.

21 That is the theological
    context of this letter. We do not set ourselves up as possessing
    superior knowledge about the state of our world or the detailed
    policies that would make it a better place. But, the church has an
    obligation to engage constructively with the political process, and
    Christians share responsibility with all citizens to participate in the
    democratic structures of our nation. We offer these reflections
    because we believe the gospel of Jesus Christ is enormously
    relevant to the questions which the coming Election will throw into
    sharp relief.

Apathy, cynicism and politics today

22 As bishops of the Church of England, we are in touch with all kinds of communities across the country through our local churches. And we maintain close links with the elected politicians for the constituencies in our dioceses. In our experience, the great majority of politicians and candidates enter politics with a passion to improve the lives of their fellow men and women. They will disagree wildly about how to achieve this, but with few exceptions, politicians are not driven merely by cynicism or self-interest. The low esteem in which politicians are held today has many roots. But simply blaming the individuals concerned is not an adequate response.

23 Turnout at General Elections since the Second World War has fallen to below two-thirds of the population. The highest turnout was in 1950 (83.9%) and the lowest was in 2001 (59.4%). At the last election in 2010, turnout

> no-one in politics today has a convincing story about a healthy balance between national government and global economic power.

only reached 65.1%. In local elections turnout has dropped far further. The declining number of people exercising their democratic right to vote reflects a worrying level of non-participation.

24 At the recent referendum on Scottish independence, the turnout was back to the level of the 1950 General Election. Why did this poll buck the trend? Perhaps because the Scottish electorate understood that the outcome would make an enormous difference to themselves, their families, their communities and their futures. It was about the possibility of a new vision of Scottish life – and Scottish politics – with all the hope and risk of such visionary innovation.

25 But in the UK as a whole, numerous polls show that a majority of people think that it will make no difference whichever party is in power. Our democracy is failing because successive administrations have done little to address the trends which are most influential in shaping ordinary people's lives.

26 The trend toward globalisation is often regarded as impossible to resist. It has brought many benefits. At the same time it has made national government more difficult, even though not all the manifestations of globalisation are inevitable, or incapable of being shaped to suit national and regional distinctiveness, as witness the differences between the politics and economies of countries with otherwise similar histories and characteristics. The problem is that no one in politics today has a convincing story about a healthy balance between national government and global economic power.

27 It is vital to find better ways of talking about many fundamental
    questions facing us today. To name only a few of the major
    questions which contemporary politics seems determined to avoid,
    we need a richer justification for the state, a better account of the
    purposes of government, and a more serious way of talking about
    taxation. Most of all, we need an honest account of how we must live
    in the future if generations yet to come are not to inherit a denuded
    and exhausted planet.

28 It is not a matter
    of ticking off these
    issues one by one in
    election manifestos
    and speeches. Decent
    answers to the questions
    facing the nation will only
    emerge when politicians
    start to promote a
    dialogue with the people about a worthwhile society, how individuals,
    communities and the nation relate to each other, and the potentials
    and limitations of politics in achieving such ends.

> Most of all, we need an honest account of how we must live in the future if generations yet to come are not to inherit a denuded and exhausted planet.

29 The different parties have failed to offer attractive visions of the
    kind of society and culture they wish to see, or distinctive goals they
    might pursue. Instead, we are subjected to sterile arguments about
    who might manage the existing system best. There is no idealism in
    this prospectus.

30 Our electoral system often means that the outcomes turn on a very small group of people within the overall electorate. Greater social mobility and the erosion of old loyalties to place or class mean that all the parties struggle to maintain their loyal core of voters whilst reaching out to those who might yet be swayed their way. The result is that any capacious political vision is stifled.

31 Instead, parties generate policies targeted at specific demographic groupings, fashioned by expediency rather than vision or even consistency. The art, or science, of targeting policies to tightly-defined electoral groups has become highly sophisticated – but the idea that politics is about satisfying the wants of distinct groups so as to win their votes has prevented our politics from rising above a kind of Dutch auction.

32 The time has surely come to move beyond mere "retail politics", where parties tailor their policies to the groups whose votes they need, regardless of the good of the majority, whilst lobbyists, pressure groups and sectional interests come armed with their policy shopping lists and judge politicians by how many items they promise to deliver. Instead of treating politics as an extension of consumerism, we should focus on the common good, the participation of more people in developing a political vision and constructive ways to talk about communities and how they relate to one another.

Visions worth voting for

33 Since the Second World War, two administrations have offered visions of society that "changed the political weather" – Clement Attlee's Labour government of 1945 and Margaret Thatcher's Conservative administration of 1979. The first responded to the discontents of the Depression in the 1930s and the socially unifying experience of the War to establish the National Health Service, to make free schooling available for all and to implement the Beveridge Report of 1942 which argued for a state welfare system to combat the "Five Giant Evils" of Want, Disease, Ignorance, Squalor and Idleness.

34 In 1979, the incoming Conservative government was pledged to facilitate individual enterprise and a market freed from state interference. Just as successive administrations between 1945 and 1979, Conservative as well as Labour, tended to regard the collectivist structures introduced under Attlee as part of a strong national consensus, so different administrations since that of Margaret Thatcher have treated the market-oriented and individualistic emphasis of her governments as part of the undisputed political landscape.

35 We are now as distant in time from Margaret Thatcher's first government as hers was from Attlee's. Both administrations changed the way people looked at society, politics, the role of government and the nature of human relationships. But today, neither vision addresses our condition.

36 One measure of the stature of these two administrations is that neither was, initially, as lacking in nuance as they have often been portrayed. William Beveridge followed his report on social security with another entitled Voluntary Action which affirmed the principles of personal responsibility and local, informal, activities which built stronger communities. He argued that the state had an important role but that it should not be allowed completely to supplant local and individual responsibility and initiative. Margaret Thatcher was, famously, keen to restore "Victorian Values", by which she meant not only unregulated markets but a strong sense of duty, self-help and personal responsibility.

> Part of our tragedy is that our politics has been incapable of holding a careful balance between different kinds of goods or virtues.

37 Part of our tragedy is that our politics has been incapable of holding a careful balance between different kinds of goods or virtues. Beveridge's enthusiasm for voluntary action was marginalised by the revolution in state welfare provision which his earlier report had initiated. Thatcher's market revolution emphasised individualism, consumerism and the importance of the corporate sector to the extent that, far from returning to Victorian notions of social responsibility, the paradigm for all relationships became competitive individualism, consumption and the commercial contract, fragmenting social solidarity at many levels.

38 Our political life would be enhanced if we could acknowledge that a modern nation, where ties of kindred and neighbourliness are often very weak, requires state-sponsored action to underpin the welfare of each citizen – but that this provision must neither supplant local voluntary action and neighbourliness where those things exist, nor ignore the way in which dependence on state provision can undermine individual initiative and responsibility. Beveridge understood that if the state is given too much power to shape society it will stifle the very voluntarism that prevents the state from being hopelessly overburdened by human need.

39 Our political life would be equally enhanced if it were possible to speak about markets, business and the profit motive as an impressively effective system of distribution in a complex society and hugely liberating of human creativity – but one which also tends to entrench inequality, diminish human sympathies and, unchecked, damage the conditions for its own flourishing. Adam Smith, the father of market economics, understood that, without a degree of shared morality which it neither creates nor sustains, the market is not protected against its in-built tendency to generate cartels and monopolies which undermine the principles of the market itself.

40   The way in which state welfare and market economics have been polarised in political debate has obscured an important point on which both Thatcher and Beveridge might well have agreed. Both understood that their approaches to the well being of the nation could not succeed unless social relationships were marked by neighbourliness, strong voluntary commitment and personal responsibility. We would add that these virtues must be practised, not just in pursuit of one's own well being, but for the flourishing of the communities in which one is set.

41   This is the missing link which has prevented the state and the market alike from generating a better, more humane, society. Placing excessive faith in state intervention on the one hand or the free market on the other, politicians have focussed so much on the things they can control directly through economic and social policy that they have neglected to nurture, by word, example or policy, those aspects of life which governments can influence but not control.

42   Adversarial politics, while necessary, has bequeathed us an adversarial approach to ideas, in which one's opponents must always be wholly wrong and criticism of one's own ideas is never legitimate. Creative attempts by politicians, mainly in periods of opposition, to challenge this trend have foundered under the pressures of day-to-day government in an unrelenting media spotlight. When it descends into tribalism, politics ceases to be about wisdom, balance or humility.

A Society of Strangers?

43 Today, a fundamental question is about the extent of social solidarity in Britain. Are we a "society of strangers", or are we a "community of communities"?

44 There is no doubt that we have become much more of a society of strangers through recent decades. That is one consequence of greatly increased physical mobility and the advance of communication technologies which allow all manner of superficial transactions without people meeting face to face.

45 But we are also a society of strangers in a more worrying sense. Consumption, rather than production, has come to define us, and individualism has tended to estrange people from one another. So has an excessive emphasis on competition regarded as a sort of social Darwinism. (This is a perverse consequence of allowing market rhetoric to creep into social policy. For an economist, competition is not the opposite of cooperation but of monopoly). Other people come to be seen first as a threat and only incidentally as a gift with the potential to enrich my life.

46 The central character in the way we discuss economics and politics today is the autonomous individual exercising choices. In our relationship with God it is true that the individual must make a response to God's

> Consumption, rather than production, has come to define us, and individualism has tended to estrange people from one another.

unconditional offer of love. But in both Old and New Testaments the words for "choice" almost never refer to the choices we make – instead they are about our experience of being chosen by God. The individualism of consumer economics and political life today makes the individual sovereign. In Christian theology, God is sovereign and the individual and the community are the focus of God's choice to love and nurture his people.

47 Because God chooses to love every human being equally, and demonstrated this love in the life, death and resurrection of Jesus, it matters when material barriers are erected which divide people and communities. When people's experiences of belonging to the nation become too different, they feel no common bond or sympathy with each other.

48 And yet we are not entirely a society of strangers. Most people still find numerous ways of belonging amongst other people – through the workplace, through voluntary associations, through shared religious and other beliefs, through shared interests, and through shared places. In each of these modes of belonging, there are solidarities, customs, and a sense of identifying with each other, without which our lives would be extraordinarily fragile and lonely. The extent of loneliness in society today, with the attendant problems of mental and physical health, is one indication of how far we have drifted into a society of strangers. But that drift is far from complete – and few people, if asked, would say that a society of strangers represents a vision of society which they desire.

> The extent of loneliness in society today, with the attendant problems of mental and physical health, is one indication of how far we have drifted into a society of strangers.

A Community of Communities

49 It would be easier for people to forge strong social bonds if we could recognise that a sense of "place" helps to form people's identity in community. Information technology may mean that physical presence is no longer necessary for many purposes. This has often been positive, and has made many kinds of human interaction easier. But people cannot so easily be uncoupled from the geographical spaces they inhabit.

> People are not so much divorced from place as seeking a place where they can be most at home.

50 People are not so much divorced from place as seeking a place where they can be most at home. Following the great rehousing boom of the 1950s and '60s, numerous studies explored the effect of dislocation on people and communities. Strong social bonds, forged in the adversity of poor housing, frequently did not translate to the new estates, despite their better conditions. And today, attempts to address the shortage of suitable housing will create new problems if they neglect people's attachment to particular places and the social networks they create there.

51 The Church of England has always had a strong commitment to place through the parish system. We are present in every community of England. We therefore see day by day how important "place" is to all kinds of people. Social policies which assume that everyone is happily mobile and footloose miss the crucial point that "place" is not just about territory but about informal networks which people build to make life sociable, neighbourly and worth living. Policies which are careless of this attachment to place do not serve people well.

> The Church of England has always had a strong commitment to place through the parish system. We are present in every community of England. We therefore see day by day how important "place" is to all kinds of people.

52 This is not about nostalgia for an old way of life, or a rejection of the modern advances which have brought us to where we are. A sensible approach to social policy will seek balance and look for correctives to those trends which, taken too far, are harmful to human flourishing. The need today is for a strong corrective to the tendency to become, more and more, a society of strangers. The corrective is likely to be found in strengthening the idea that our nation is still, to a useful degree, a community of communities.

53 One important principle here is the idea of subsidiarity – the principle that decisions should be devolved to the lowest level consistent with effectiveness. Subsidiarity derives from Catholic social teaching, and it is a good principle for challenging the accumulation of power in fewer and fewer hands. It does not mean that everything must be devolved to the most local level. Nor is it about handing small matters downward whilst retaining all meaningful authority in the hands of the powerful. It does entail careful attention to the areas of life where we function best as a nation and other areas where people function best as members of something smaller and more local.

> If people feel part of the decision-making processes that affect their lives, there is no reason why, in many aspects of social policy, local diversity should not flourish.

54 As an example, "post code lottery" has become a term of disparagement for local variations in public services. But that implies that a single standard, determined and enforced nationally, is the only way to order every aspect of public life. It is certainly true that many services should be available as equally as possible to every citizen. But it is also true that different communities have different needs and may choose different priorities. If people feel part of the decision-making processes that affect their lives, there is no reason why, in many aspects of social policy, local diversity should not flourish.

55 The desire for neatness, as much as the desire for control, is characteristic of how politicians tend to think – especially those in government or contemplating office. They are often backed up by bureaucracies which are allergic to messiness. But human life and creativity are inherently messy and rebel against the uniformity that accompanies systemic constraints and universal solutions.

56 Whether on the political right or the political left, it is a long time since there has been a coherent policy programme which made a virtue of dispersing power and control as widely across the population as possible. We have been offered salvation through the state and salvation through the market. Both emphases help clarify things that are true about the human condition, but neither tells an adequate story. Both have taken power and decision-making away from the levels of human interaction where people feel most able to become human together.

57 Unless a political vision emerges which reaffirms the bonds which tie us together as a nation, as localities, as communities and as neighbours, we shall be left with the spectacle of politicians claiming more and more powers and yet achieving less and less that is worthwhile.

The Person in Community

58 Our hope for a stronger politics of community is driven by the conviction, founded on experience and evidence, that individuals flourish best when they belong with confidence to networks of relationships, institutions and communities which extend well beyond the nuclear family but stop well short of the state or the corporation.

59 We are most human when we know ourselves to be dependent on others. That is something we first learn in families, if we are fortunate enough to experience the blessings of family life. And families are not only for children. They are also about making old age creative and happy. Nor are families completely self-contained units. They flourish best when there are networks of friendship, neighbourliness and mutual support around them. Our society celebrates the autonomy of individuals but does too little to acknowledge that dependency on others is what makes human beings social creatures.

60 Paradoxically, too much stress on the individual, and on the supposedly autonomous choices of the individual-as-consumer, has tended to diminish rather than enhance the moral significance of each unique person. It has led us to undervalue individuals who exhibit weakness, are dependent on others, or who try to live selflessly. When individuality is thought to stem from autonomy and freedom of choice, a particular image of the ideal individual – young, free, attractive, and materially comfortable – becomes the archetype against which everyone is measured and most are found wanting.

61 Most people, when asked, subscribe to some version of the idea that all people are created equal. Yet this is contradicted in the way that some categories of people are spoken about – people who are sick, disabled, terminally ill or otherwise unable to live the life that a consumer society celebrates; people who are unable to work, materially poor or mentally ill in ways which challenge "acceptable" ways of being unwell.

> There is a deep contradiction in the attitudes of a society which celebrates equality in principle yet treats some people, especially the poor and vulnerable, as unwanted, unvalued and unnoticed.

62 There is a deep contradiction in the attitudes of a society which celebrates equality in principle yet treats some people, especially the poor and vulnerable, as unwanted, unvalued and unnoticed. It is particularly counter-productive to denigrate those who are in need, because this undermines the wider social instinct to support one another in the community. For instance, when those who rely on social security payments are all described in terms that imply they are undeserving, dependent, and ought to be self-sufficient, it deters others from offering the informal, neighbourly support which could ease some of the burden of welfare on the state.

63 This is why it is important to move away from the focus on the individual to a richer narrative of the person in community. If, as they say, it takes a village to raise a child, then the single mother who cannot face the stresses of motherhood alone need not fear isolation or carry an impossible burden. If the care of severely disabled people, the terminally ill or people with dementia was shared in the context of a supportive network of friends, neighbours and allies, the fear of being a burden on others would not lead so many to undervalue their own life, even to the point of seeking to end it.

> It is vital to move beyond the superficial equality of free consumers in a market place of relationships and to see the virtues in the relationships of family and community which are given, not chosen.

64 Restoring the balance between the individual and the community around them is a necessity if every person is to be truly valued for who they are and not just on a crude calculus of utility. It is vital to move beyond the superficial equality of free consumers in a market place of relationships and to see the virtues in the relationships of family and community which are given, not chosen.

The community of nations

65 Like the relationships of persons in community, relationships between nations and peoples are shaped by more than economic interests alone. Good relationships take into account the power of history and the history of power. The enduring memories of old wrongs, and the affinities that come from shared experiences and cultures can make or break today's international relations. Global power is as unevenly distributed as global wealth and yet good international relations require all nations to recognise their interdependence if the world is to remain stable or even to survive.

> World trade has demonstrated how intertwined the national economy is with other nations'. But our perceptions of cultural and political interdependence lag far behind.

66 Just as the myth of personal autonomy distorts human communities, so the illusion that a nation can flourish without strong international alliances distorts the bigger picture of our shared humanity. World trade has demonstrated how intertwined the national economy is with other nations'. But our perceptions of cultural and political interdependence lag far behind.

67 After the Second World War, the nations of Europe sought to rebuild for prosperity through a shared determination that never again would global neighbours resort to mass slaughter. The differences between the peoples of Europe, which had loomed so large in war, seemed insignificant when people recollected how extensively they shared a history, culture and, not least, the traditions and world views of the Christian faith. English churchmen worked tirelessly to promote understanding and cooperation between the European churches and to encourage the political institutions of the European nations to work for the common good and focus on what they shared, not what divided them.

68 That history is not an argument for the structures and institutions of the European Union as they now exist. But it is an enduring argument for continuing to build structures of trust and cooperation between the nations of Europe. Ignoring or denying the extent to which European people share culture and heritage suggests that questions of identity and belonging have no currency except as political bargaining chips.

69 If there is a threat to the values and institutions of our nation, it does not come today from our closest neighbours in Europe. The volatile areas of the world, where conflict or the threat of war seem endemic, are a constant threat to the stability of all nations – another reminder of our interdependence.

70 Military intervention by states such as Britain is not always wrong.
    But recent experiences, especially in Iraq and Afghanistan, show the
    difficulty of treading a line between legitimate defence of human
    values and interventions which further destabilise regions already
    devastated by conflict. We have discovered how acute is the risk of
    generating new resentments which intensify the threat to our own
    way of life.

71 The decision to commit
    troops to war is one of
    the hardest which any
    politician has to take
    and those who bear that
    responsibility deserve our
    constant prayers. And the
    nation should value and
    pray for military personnel
    who know that their lives

> We have discovered
> how acute is the risk
> of generating new
> resentments which
> intensify the threat to our
> own way of life.

depend on the wisdom and judgement of politicians. But our support
should not be offered blindly. Our politicians have been reluctant
to talk openly with the electorate about Britain's relationships
around the world, the realignments of global power, a realistic role in
securing a stable and peaceful world order and the tools we would
need for the job. In short, we should reflect more deeply on Britain's
role in generating an international community of communities.

72 The sheer scale of indiscriminate destructive power represented by nuclear weapons such as Trident was only justifiable, if at all, by appeal to the principle of mutually assured destruction. For many, including many Christians, that in itself was a deeply problematic argument, although there were also many who were prepared to live with the strategy because it appeared to secure peace and save lives. Shifts in the global strategic realities mean that the traditional arguments for nuclear deterrence need re-examining. The presence of such destructive capacity pulls against any international sense of shared community. But such is the talismanic power of nuclear weaponry that few politicians seem willing to trust the electorate with a real debate about the military capacity we need in the world of today.

73 Reconciliation between divided peoples is at the heart of a Christian commitment to the world, just as it is the key to our understandings of community and society. People and nations are divided, not just by military conflict but by grotesque inequalities of wealth and power. The accumulation of wealth and power in the hands of a few nations has a profoundly destabilising effect.

74 Supporting developing nations without creating unhealthy dependencies is politically challenging and yet absolutely necessary. The government is to be commended for committing 0.7% of GDP to overseas aid when budgets have been so hard pressed. For any party to abandon or reduce this commitment would be globally irresponsible in pragmatic terms as well as indicating that the moral imperatives of mutuality and reconciliation counted for nothing.

Equality – us and them

75 Inequality, whether global or national, can develop quickly but take a long time to overcome. In Britain, material inequality continues to widen. We have become again the kind of nation which the Conservative leader, Disraeli, deplored: "Two nations between whom there is no intercourse and no sympathy; who are as ignorant of each other's habits, thoughts, and feelings as if they were dwellers in different zones, or inhabitants of different planets. The rich and the poor."

76 Parties of the extreme right and extreme left have sometimes sought to rekindle the language of class – but by trying to tap into class resentments rather than

> Inequality, whether global or national, can develop quickly but take a long time to overcome.

speaking of the warmer virtues of mutuality and solidarity. Stirring up resentment against some identifiable "other" always dehumanises some social group or people. Ethnic minorities, immigrants, welfare claimants, bankers and oligarchs – all have been called up as threats to some fictitious "us". They become the hated "other" without whose presence among us all would be well. It is a deep irony that the whole political class is often regarded as an alien "other" by many sectors of the population.

77 At first sight, the rhetoric of "us" and "the other" may sound as if it is talking about communities and significant social groupings – the opposite of individualistic politics. In reality, it represents no actual class or community but appeals to the individual's ignorance of those who are different. It is the political mirror-image of the major parties' failure to generate a more appealing political narrative – the image in the glass seems to be the reverse of the dominant political story, but there is nothing distinctive or new there.

> At first sight, the rhetoric of "us" and "the other" may sound as if it is talking about communities and significant social groupings... In reality, it represents no actual class or community but appeals to the individual's ignorance of those who are different.

Strengthening institutions

78 Our focus on stronger communities is about building a commitment to the long term and the kind of trust in each other that allows the future to be something for "us" and not just "me" – a world for our grandchildren as well as ourselves

79 Because a society centred on individuals finds trust difficult, laws, regulations and contracts have entered into many areas of life that were once governed by shared understandings of ethics and wisdom. When law and regulation intrude too far into everyday life, they create a "chill factor" where anxiety about the rules prevents people acting freely, sensibly or with wisdom, even in areas which are not, in fact, governed by official regulations.

80 For instance, laws such as those about health and safety were created for a good purpose. But the common perception of "health and safety gone mad" may reflect an exaggerated fear that ordinary life is now governed by rules which seem to be enforced without regard for common sense. When people work together within a common culture, it becomes possible to trust in their shared wisdom and to avoid assuming that everyone is a fool or a knave who must be constrained by regulations and protocols.

81 This is another reason why we need new, informal and independent structures, small enough not to need every activity to be codified, through which we can learn to work together in trust, not just according to rules. Such bodies – often called intermediate institutions – are a lot bigger than the family but far smaller than the state.

82 The churches are among the most historically embedded and well-established of the intermediate institutions, and remain among the most effective, so we are naturally keen to see the contribution of the churches to society, culture and the nation recognised and supported. But our concern goes far beyond self-interest. A thriving society needs many intermediate institutions, including those who disagree with each other and pursue incompatible goals. A culture in good order needs that kind of diversity and capacity to argue about what makes a good society.

83 Intermediate institutions are too often overlooked by policy-makers, so they struggle to be as influential and beneficial as they might. Housing Associations are a good example. So are Credit Unions which offer a source of responsible saving and credit which could be an ethical alternative to many of the activities of the discredited banks and the mistrusted pay day lenders. Credit Unions and Housing Associations both draw on the principle of mutuality. Both are good at serving less well off people, although neither is solely for the poor or best understood as an anti-poverty measure. Indeed, both Credit Unions and Housing Associations work best when there is "buy in" from a broad social spectrum. They are institutions with a strong unifying potential.

84 We are living through both a banking crisis and a housing crisis. The Archbishop of Canterbury is actively championing Credit Unions, as is the Government's Credit Union Expansion Programme. Institutions like Credit Unions and Housing Associations are not important simply because they are effective but because they embody the principle of mutuality – the common bond between people being the heart of the operation and not just a bolt-on accessory.

> The purpose of education is not simply to prepare people to be economic units but to nurture their ability to flourish as themselves and to seek the flourishing of others.

85 Our educational institutions – especially schools, with their vocation to be distinctive and inclusive – also do much to foster a community of communities. A good school nurtures each child, respecting their individuality and the traditions and customs – including the religious faith – in which they are growing up in their family, whilst introducing them to the practices of living among others with different backgrounds and histories. The purpose of education is not simply to prepare people to be economic units but to nurture their ability to flourish as themselves and to seek the flourishing of others.

86 Long before the provision of free state schooling for all, Church of England schools sought to make a liberal education available to all children, and not just those growing up in the Christian faith. This work continues today.

87 It is a fallacy to believe that a community of communities can be built from a position of assumed neutrality – everybody is rooted somewhere. Acknowledging one's own roots and traditions is a first step toward respecting and understanding the roots and traditions of others. That is the vision which Church of England schools, like the church more widely, seek to promote. All schools should try to model a community of communities and not a society of strangers.

> Acknowledging one's own roots and traditions is a first step toward respecting and understanding the roots and traditions of others.

Disagreement, Diversity and Coalitions

88 In Britain, we have become so used to believing that self-interest drives every decision that it takes a leap of imagination to argue that there should be stronger institutions for those we disagree with as well as for those "on our side". Breaking free of self-interest and welcoming our opponents as well as our supporters into a messy, noisy, yet rich and creative community of communities is, perhaps, the only way we will enrich our almost-moribund political culture.

89 The Church of England locally and nationally, has learned how to build constructive alliances with other voluntary agencies, charities and community groups. The fallacy that people can only work together if they agree about every issue is proved wrong day after day. It is precisely this ability to make, and break, alliances – so that people can work together on issues they share, but may not be on the same side on other issues – which makes intermediate institutions, and the voluntary sector generally, so crucial to a flourishing democratic society.

> The Church of England locally and nationally, has learned how to build constructive alliances with other voluntary agencies, charities and community groups.

Beyond "Left" and "Right"

90 Our country is hungry for a new approach to political life that will
    "change the political weather" as decisively as did the administrations
    of 1945 and 1979. We need a new political story that will enable
    the people of Britain to articulate who they are, what they want to
    become and how they will work together to live virtuously as well as
    prosperously.

91 No such thing is yet on
    offer for 2015, though
    this may be an election
    that sows the seeds from
    which a new narrative
    might emerge. Or it may
    be an election which
    confirms people in
    cynicism and despair and
    sows a very different sort

> We are seeking, not a
> string of policy offers,
> but a way of ordering our
> political and economic life
> which can be pursued in
> a conservative idiom, a
> socialist idiom, a liberal
> idiom – and by others.

    of seed from which may grow a tree of conflict, unrest and division.

92 It will already be clear that we do not see the way forward as a
    choice between "right" and "left". Nor are we trying to split the
    difference, imagining that the truth lies equidistant between
    extremes. We are emphasising an approach to politics which can
    trace its roots on both left and right and which could be embraced
    by any of the mainstream parties without being untrue to their own
    histories.

93 Different parties will disagree about how best to put similar ideas into practice. We are seeking, not a string of policy offers, but a way of conceiving and ordering our political and economic life which can be pursued in a conservative idiom, a socialist idiom, a liberal idiom – and by others not aligned to party.

94 Before, and immediately after, the 2010 General Election, this kind of new political thinking was briefly prominent in the concept of The Big Society. The idea came from thoughtful Conservatives who had used the years of opposition to conceive a better political approach than what had gone before, and one which was derived very clearly from an earlier Conservative tradition.

95 The Church of England strongly supported The Big Society. We saw that the philosophy it represented commanded support from well beyond the Conservative party. The title of the project is not what matters. The time may not have been ripe for the ideas to be translated into practical policies. But the ideals that The Big Society stood for should not be consigned to the political dustbin – they could still be the foundation for the new approach to politics, economics and community which we seek.

96 On both sides of the house, in the Commons and in the Lords, there are members who broadly share the perspective we have outlined here. More work along similar lines is being done in think-tanks, academic groups, and among some journalists and local activists. But, so far, these discussions have been confined to the margins. We aim here to push those ideas toward the centre of political conversation.

History in an old country

97 The United Kingdom has evolved over the centuries. It has no written constitution. Institutions of all kinds have tended to evolve and adapt rather than being destroyed and rebuilt. That is not to argue that all our constitutional and political structures are fit for purpose today. But governments will always tend to prefer structures which accumulate more power to themselves – and oppositions will collude with this in the hope that their turn in power will come – leaving ordinary people increasingly powerless.

98 The aftermath of the recent Scottish referendum has thrown the constitutional arrangements of the UK into sharp focus. The idea that the future shape of the Union and the relationship between its constituents can be solved in weeks or months is a fine example of politics ignoring the importance of history in favour of the calculated advantages of the moment. It is a mirage to think there is a single, logical and fool-proof structure which could be designed on a clean sheet of paper.

99 The impatience of politicians or the desire for party advantage must not be the driver for constitutional changes. There should be the widest possible consultation about the structures and constitution we need, in which as many people participate as possible, and where the lessons of history (and not just British history) are kept sharply in view. A good constitution will maximise the involvement of as many people as possible in the decisions that shape their country, their neighbourhood and their family.

Power, identities and minorities

100 One recurring theme of this letter is the need to combat the accumulations of power which leave too many people powerless. We need a more subtle way of understanding power in society – and its disparities.

101 But who counts as "we"? It is impossible to ignore the question "who is my neighbour?" It is a question familiar to anyone who has ever picked up a New Testament. But it is also a question that arises implicitly and explicitly in the fraught politics of migration and identity.

> One recurring theme of this letter is the need to combat the accumulations of power which leave too many people powerless.

102 In the gospel, the question "who is my neighbour?" led Jesus to recount the parable of the Good Samaritan. Jesus makes two subtle points, first calling people to follow the example of the Samaritan, the foreigner who went to the aid of the wounded traveller; and secondly, answering the question by suggesting that neighbourliness may mean receiving care from a member of a despised social group. Neighbourliness, then, is not just about what we do for others. It is also about what we are willing to receive from those we fear, ignore or despise.

103 The politics of migration has, too often, been framed in crude terms of "us" and "them" with scant regard for the Christian traditions of neighbourliness and hospitality. The way we talk about migration, with ethnically identifiable communities being treated as "the problem" has, deliberately or inadvertently, created an ugly undercurrent of racism in every debate about immigration. Crude stereotyping is incompatible with a Christian understanding of human social relationships.

104 But we also challenge the assumption that to question immigration at all must always be racist. Major trends in migration have brought about immense social changes in many parts of the country. Rapid change has often impacted most acutely on communities which are least equipped to handle it – partly because their experience has often been that change is to their detriment.

105 It is unsurprising that communities which have faced deindustrialisation, the destruction of familiar streets and housing, whose pride in work and craftsmanship has been destroyed by the shift from manufacturing to services and for whom poverty has never been more than one step away should find the rapid shift to a multicultural society difficult to assimilate. Suspicion of people with other national and ethnic origins needs to be understood without being endorsed or excused. We need a dialogue about migration which ceases to use people as political cyphers and looks instead at who is being asked to bear the cost of rapid social change and what resources of community and neighbourliness they need to emerge stronger from change.

Debt and a humane economy

106 The last Parliament has been dominated by the after shocks of the economic and financial crisis of 2008. It is to the credit of our politicians that the impact of the crisis has been less severe in Britain than in some other European countries. It is to the discredit of our politicians that a financial catastrophe which threatened the stability of the world at large has become a political football rather than a concerted effort to bring the nation through the crisis with as much of its social fabric as possible intact.

107 It is game-playing to claim that anyone who cares about the impact of austerity on the most vulnerable members of society is, by definition, careless about the extent of national indebtedness. The mirror image of that view is equally trivialising: a concern to reduce indebtedness need not necessitate grinding the faces of the poor. Debts, whether national or personal, are rarely good news. Indebtedness means handing power over one's life to the creditor – widespread indebtedness is another manifestation of the accumulation of power in too few hands. This is as true for nations as for individuals and families.

108 When the financial crisis first broke, the General Synod debated the likely impact. The prospect of years of austerity was obvious even then. But the Synod set down three criteria by which any austerity measure ought to be judged.

109 They were: Is it fair? Does it give priority to the vulnerable – the young struggling to enter the labour market, and the elderly living on fixed incomes; people in poverty both within Britain and globally? Is it generous? Does it embody the obligation to give and share our resources with others, especially those less well off? Does it promote fair trade and global aid? Is it sustainable? Have the medium and long-term implications been taken fully into account so that the interests of our children's and grandchildren's generations are factored in?

110 These three principles are in tension with each other and have to be balanced together. They remain sound criteria for judging how the present government's debt-reduction policies have fared in practice. They are useful questions to put to candidates who will stand before the electorate in the coming months. It has been widely observed that the greatest burdens of austerity have not been born by those with the broadest shoulders – that is, those who enjoy a wide buffer zone before they fall into real need. Those whose margin of material security was always narrow have not been adequately protected from the impact of recession.

111 It is good that unemployment has not risen as high as was predicted, or as high as past experience suggested it would. Worklessness has long been acknowledged as corrosive of human dignity and sense of identity.

112 But instead we have seen the burgeoning of in-work poverty – people who, despite working hard, cannot earn enough to live decently. The market can, and does, allow wages to rise and fall in response to demand and supply. But human lives are not infinitely flexible in the way the price mechanism expects, and people cannot live properly when their work brings in too little to sustain dignity.

113 This is why the Church of England has backed the concept of the Living Wage – an agreement with employers to ensure that all their staff earn a modest hourly rate that is sufficient for a full time worker to live decently. The Archbishop of York has been at the forefront in arguing for the Living Wage. It represents the basic principle that people are not commodities and that their lives cannot adapt infinitely in response to market pressures. The labour market cannot enable people to live and flourish unless the moral limits of the market are recognised.

114 When people live as part of a community and can depend upon one another, the moral limits of markets become clearer. This kind of community does not even need to rely on personal acquaintance, only on a perception of mutual reliance. In the maritime industry, shipping companies compete against each other in an open market. But when a ship is in trouble, it is unthinkable that other ships in the vicinity will not go to its assistance, at considerable commercial cost. Those who make their living on the sea know their need of each other. For the rest of us, our mutual dependence is no less real, but is often obscured from our sight until troubles arise.

Our grandchildren's future

115 Our grandchildren's future, not just the wants of the moment, must be factored into economic and political priorities. When prosperity – and, for the least well off, survival – appears to depend more on luck than merit and when rewards seem divorced from virtue, there is no incentive to invest in a future we will not ourselves enjoy. Why build the foundations of the next generation's future if it could be swept away by the throw of the economic dice?

116 This shows why economics must be understood as a moral discipline. A thriving economy needs investors who look to the long term. But when the economy has pursued short term profit and stopped thinking long term, people's rational behaviour follows suit. It is hard to promote virtuous living when the shape of the economy sends a very different message about human responsibility.

> Our grandchildren's future, not just the wants of the moment, must be factored into economic and political priorities.

117 People will commit to the long term if they have a stake in it. Intergenerational justice depends upon sharing power and decision making now. By enabling people to build a stake in the communities they are encouraged to live, not only for the day, but for their grandchildren's future – and, on behalf of future generations, to cherish the created order rather than viewing our environment as a commodity to be consumed.

The campaign ahead

118 The election campaign is likely to entrench the apathy and cynicism with which many people approach politics today. To accept such attitudes is a counsel of despair. Unless we exercise the democratic rights that our ancestors struggled for, we will share responsibility for the failures of the political classes. It is the duty of every Christian adult to vote, even though it may have to be a vote for something less than a vision that inspires us.

119 If the country is ever to enjoy a new politics which reflects our beliefs about human flourishing, we must work with others to make that vision attractive, imagine how it might be made real and help those with a vocation to political life to argue for better ways of doing things.

120 At this election, we can sow the seeds of a new politics. We encourage voters to support candidates and policies which demonstrate the following key values:
- Halting and reversing the accumulation of power and wealth in fewer and fewer hands, whether those of the state, corporations or individuals.
- Involving people at a deeper level in the decisions that affect them most.
- Recognising the distinctive communities, whether defined by geography, religion or culture, which make up the nation and enabling all to thrive and participate together.
- Treating the electorate as people with roots, commitments and

traditions and addressing us all in terms of the common good and not just as self-interested consumers.

- Demonstrating that the weak, the dependent, the sick, the aged and the vulnerable are persons of equal value to everybody else.
- Offering the electorate a grown up debate about Britain's place in the world order and the possibilities and obligations that entails.

121 We believe that these points are crucial if politics is to rise above its present diminished state. Indeed, we can develop those ideas further. In July 2014, the General Synod debated how the church contributes to The Common Good. That debate suggested some further signs that political policies were moving in the direction which this letter outlines. They included:

- Acknowledging the depth of insecurity and anxiety that has permeated our society after decades of rapid change, not least the changes brought about by the banking crisis and austerity programme.
- Recognising people's need for supportive local communities and that the informal and voluntary sectors hold society together in ways which neither the state nor private enterprise can match.
- Recognising that people need a sense of place and of belonging.
- Addressing the culture of regulation and litigation when it acts as a "chill factor" on voluntary involvement, where anxiety about potential litigation can be a brake on local action.
- Reflecting the obligation to secure the common good of future generations, not just our own, and addressing issues of intergenerational justice. This must include a responsible approach to environmental issues.

122 All election campaigns are hard fought and rightly so. It is at the heart of our democratic process that people hold candidates to account, cutting beneath the jargon and "on-message" glibness

> This letter is about building a vision of a better kind of world, a better society and better politics.

which has come to characterise political language. Candidates who free themselves from clichés and party formulae may be showing the first signs of that human sympathy which would enable them to be real representatives of their constituents rather than simply needing our votes to gain power.

123 This letter is about building a vision of a better kind of world, a better society and better politics. Underlying those ideas is the concept of virtue – what it means to be a good person, a good politician, a good neighbour or a good community. Virtues are nourished, not by atomised individualism, but in strong communities which relate honestly and respectfully to other groups and communities which make up this nation.

124 Strong communities are schools of virtue – they are the places where we learn how to be good, how to live well and how to make relationships flourish. They build on the traditions through which each generation learns its national, local and family identity. Virtues are ways of living that can be learned, but which too many trends in recent decades have eroded.

125 Religious traditions like the Christian faith try to be repositories of virtue – ways for people to learn who they are, how they relate to each other and how they deal with difference and disagreement.

The religious life is not just grounded on belief in God – it is grounded in practices of prayer and service, through which people learn to reflect on the deep nature of themselves, others and the world at large, under God, and work together for greater human flourishing.

> The religious life is not just grounded on belief in God – it is grounded in practices of prayer and service, through which people learn to reflect on the deep nature of themselves, others and the world at large, under God, and work together for greater human flourishing.

126 The advice of St Paul in his letter to the Philippians may help to defend us against the temptations of apathy, cynicism and blame, and instead seek – because we are disciples of Jesus Christ who long for a more humane society – a better politics for a better nation.

Whatever is true, whatever is honourable, whatever is just, whatever is pure, whatever is pleasing, whatever is commendable, if there is any excellence and if there is anything worthy of praise, think about these things.

Published on behalf of the House of Bishops by

Church House Publishing
Church House
Great Smith Street
London SW1P 3AZ

ISBN 0 7151 4694 1

A downloadable version of this booklet is available via
www.churchofengland.org/GeneralElection2015

Designed and printed by www.penguinboy.net
Reprinted 2015